Lincoln Christian College

P9-CFY-992

and you
visited me

and you

A guide for lay visitors to the sick

visited me

by CARL J. SCHERZER

FORTRESS PRESS

PHILADELPHIA

Biblical quotations are from the Revised Standard Version of the Bible, copyrighted 1946 and 1952 by the Division of Christian Education of the National Council of the Churches of Christ in the United States of America.

© 1966 BY FORTRESS PRESS

Library of Congress Catalog Card Number 66-24860

3425F66   Printed in U. S. A.   UB67

DEDICATED

to our grandchildren

Todd,

Bill,

Sharon,

Heidi

44749

Contents

Introduction

Visiting the sick is a custom that dates from antiquity. It is mentioned by Jesus as a praiseworthy act (Matt. 25:36), and as an example of a good deed to be practiced by his followers.

Church groups, fraternal organizations, civic clubs, in fact, almost any of all the countless organizations of our culture, appoint a "sick committee." The members of these committees are charged with the obligation to visit the sick members and to express in an appropriate manner the concern of the group for the welfare of the patient. Relatives and friends want to demonstrate their love or concern. The sick call is an effective means for doing this.

There are those who feel particularly called by God to visit and convert the sick. When a visitor with this intention told me, "God has laid it on my heart to bring conviction to the sick," I informed her that some patients had complained about her intrusion into their privacy. These "dedicated" visitors usually make their hospital calls in pairs and one or both may approach the patient with the question, "Are you saved?" or "Do you accept Jesus as your personal Savior?" They frequently distribute tracts with such titles as "What If You Should Die at Midnight?" or "Where Will You Spend Eternity?"

There are those who would not think of calling upon a sick person confined to his home. Once they learn of an acquaintance who is hospitalized, however, they feel obligated to pay a visit. If the weather is threatening, the visit can be postponed until it "gets nice outside." In consequence, when the weather is favorable the hospitalized patient may have far too many visitors; when it is inclement, none at all.

There are those visitors who consider it their self-appointed duty to visit all the patients on a particular ward or unit of the hospital, whether they know them or not. More often than not, these people create a problem for busy hospital personnel, and confuse the patient who tries to understand why a stranger called, and at whose behest.

When our Lord spoke of visiting the sick as a good deed, the reference was more inclusive than our present day concept of the "sick call." In Jesus' day, people did not have the conveniences and comforts familiar to us. Visitors to the sick demonstrated their love and concern by caring for any children in the home, preparing and serving meals, cleaning the house, and doing any needed chores. I can recall when one would not think of calling upon a sick person empty-handed. Broth, a cake, home-baked bread, or any gift of immediate practical value was taken along to give to the sick one or members of the family. The visitor was expected to remain, if needed, to help with house cleaning, preparation of meals, and so forth. In such a manner, the words of love and concern came to fruition.

Today, the practical aspects have largely been eliminated, even when the call is made in a home. The care of the hospitalized patient is supervised by professionals and there is virtually no need to bring food or plan to remain so as to assist in the physical care of the sick one.

The single aspect of the original call that remains constant is the expression of comforting words, genuine concern, and the reassurance that the ill person is an important member of a fellowship. The expression of love and comfort is limited almost entirely to words, either verbal or printed. A gift of flowers, a book, or a small basket of fruit may serve as a more tangible alternate to demonstrate the visitor's love and concern.

During many years as a hospital chaplain I have observed thousands of visitors as they called on the sick. Most of their calls were appreciated and helpful. But in far too many instances, well-meaning but tactless people were a disturbing influence. Many never realized the damage they had done. On the brighter side, it is also true that many visitors will never know the degree to which their thoughtfulness was appreciated.

On one occasion I encountered an elderly man in a hospital corridor. Because of his puzzled expression, I inquired, "May I help you; I am the chaplain."

"Yes," he replied. "In what room is Joe ———?"

"He is here in this room," I said. "Come with me and I'll take you to him."

As the visitor approached the bed, he took a long, silent look and said, "My God, Joe, are you still alive?"

In another situation I could not help but overhear a woman visitor graphically relate the details of her husband's death. (He had died suddenly of a heart attack and was pronounced dead on arrival at the hospital.) The caller wept as she continued to relate her sad story and the patient soon was also shedding tears. On another occasion, a well-meaning woman visitor related the experience of a patient who had undergone the same operation eighteen months ago and had not had a well day since.

These are but a few examples of *harmful* calls. They need not be considered as unusually tactless. Anyone who has ever been hospitalized may recall worse examples of visitation by well-meaning people. By definition, the word "visitation" *may* mean "an affliction or punishment, an unpleasant experience." In some instances the sick visit may result in that kind of a "visitation."

People visit the sick because they desire to be helpful to the patient by their expression of love and concern. This book is the result of my observation of thousands of visitors. It is intended to help the layman make his or her call upon the sick a pleasant experience both for the patient and the visitor himself.

1. Rules for Calling on the Sick

The following rules are offered as suggestions to increase the effectiveness of the visit, whether the call is made in the home, the hospital, or a nursing home. Calling upon the elderly is not our immediate concern here, although many of the suggestions apply equally well to such situations. Most of the calls are made upon fellow members of organizations and churches, friends, acquaintances, and relatives who are temporarily incapacitated by sickness, not necessarily of a terminal nature.

1. **Plan the call** when it is convenient for the patient.

Because of hospital routine, rest periods, tests, therapy, and similar reasons, the visitor may not be able to see the patient. A calling card should be left for delivery to the patient. Some visitors may prefer to pen a brief message on note paper. If the patient is busy, or visitors are excluded, the caller may leave a short message to be given to the sick one at a more convenient time.

When calling at a home, the time should be limited to the later morning or afternoon hours. These hours are usually more convenient for the patient and for members of the family who have the care of the sick one.

1

Hospitals usually restrict visiting hours because of patient care. Some hospitals try to distribute the visitor load by permitting callers any time between 10:00 a.m. and 8:00 p.m. However, if the visitor comes before 10:30 a.m. the patient may be "busy."

With the exception of the nearest of kin, it is not advisable for a patient to be disturbed by callers on the day of an operation. It is also always disturbing to interrupt a patient's meal. No one likes to dine with someone watching each bite that is taken. Older people, particularly, resent having their routine disturbed. Mealtime should be avoided in planning one's call.

The patient may desire and need to rest after the lunch period, inasmuch as the hospital routine begins with an early awakening. The most convenient hours to schedule one's hospital visits are the periods from 2:00 to 4:00 p.m. and 6:30 to 8:00 p.m. This schedule would apply equally well to calls made in a home.

2. **Be poised and calm** when entering the sick room.

The visitor should be concerned about and alert to the feelings of the patient and be in a position to adjust to them.

A middle-aged lady visitor said, "I always enter a sick room with a smile on my face and exude health and happiness." It is doubtful if a sick person would appreciate such an approach. The patient may be feeling miserable and resent such a show of health and happiness. The visitor with an overendowment of vim and vigor may unknowingly arouse feelings of envy in the patient. It is far better to enter the room as one would in making a social call; that is, with a neutral

2

mood that can be adjusted to the feelings of the one who is visited.

After the greeting, the patient will usually say, "How are you?" This is a polite exchange of pleasantry that should not be seized by the visitor as an opportunity to share his own ills, aches, and pains. It is advisable to respond casually, "I am fine. How are you?" The patient's reply will give the visitor the clue to the mood to which adjustment can be made.

3. **Shake hands,** if the patient takes the initiative.

It is inadvisable to enter a sick room with outstretched hand. The patient is thereby left without a choice in the matter. In some instances it may be painful for the patient to shake hands. Anyone with a coronary disability should avoid this strain. Embarrassment can be prevented, if the visitor will momentarily pause until the patient can indicate whether the handshake is appropriate.

When the patient so desires, the greeting may be done in a normal, natural manner. Care should be given so as not to jar or hurt the sick one with excessive pressure or motion. Once the handshake is over, the visitor should relinquish the patient's hand. It is taken for granted that there is no handshaking when either the visitor or the patient has a communicable disease. If the caller has a cold or virus infection, the visit should not have been made in the first place and shaking hands is taboo.

4. **Stand** where the patient can see
the caller comfortably.

The patient will want to see the face of the caller.

If the patient is obliged to turn in an awkward position, the effort may be painful. It is better for the visitor to walk around the bed, without touching it, to the patient's best vantage point. This applies particularly to postoperative cases, to patients with bone fractures, and victims of accidents where many muscles and tendons are sore and irritated.

5. **Be seated** only if invited to do so.

When the patient does not ask the visitor to be seated it may imply that there is pain or discomfort. The patient may be tired and in need of rest. In such a situation the call will be more appreciated if the visitor expresses concern and suggests that a visit will be made at a later date when the patient is better.

When the visitor is seated, precautions should be taken to avoid breathing into the patient's face or inhaling his breath. A call should *never* be made by a person who has a respiratory infection or even a common cold. The patient has enough with which to contend without the additional affliction left by a well-meaning visitor.

In this connection, the visitor should also be cautioned about bad breath and strong perfumes. Either or both odors can be obnoxious to one who may already be feeling a bit nauseated.

6. **Touch not** the bed; do not jar the patient.

This directive is given for various reasons. The most obvious one is that it may be unpleasant for the patient to be jarred. The visitor may have germs on the hands that can be left on the bed linens. Should the patient have an infection it could be transmitted to a visitor who touches the bed.

Under no circumstances should a visitor, even a husband or wife, sit on the patient's bed. This is particularly potentially dangerous for a patient who had an operation. Various germs accumulate in the fabric of a suit or a dress and may be deposited on the linens when a visitor sits on the bed.

If there are insufficient chairs for the visitors present in the room, the caller should express a word of greeting and then leave. Hospital rooms provide limited space for visitors to sit, and this space planning has its purpose. The presence of too many visitors tires and excites the sick one. If there are two or more already in the room, the visitor should plan to call again at a more opportune time.

7. **Speak naturally**
unless the patient has defective hearing.

The tone of voice should be neither too loud or too soft. A loud voice may be especially irritating to the sick person. The sense organs frequently become hypersensitive during periods of sickness. One with a headache, for example, will be hurt by a noise that would not otherwise be disturbing. When the visitor notices that the patient must strain to hear, the voice should be raised to a level that can be heard with comfort.

8. **Do not diagnose**
the patient's sickness or prescribe medication.

"I felt just like you do and the doctor couldn't find out what was wrong for weeks. You know what it was? It was . . . and I'll bet that's what's wrong with you."

"I took the same pills, but they did not help me. Then

I went to Dr. —— and he prescribed these. I'll bet these would get you well."

Doctors require the facilities of laboratories to diagnose, and years of intensive training before they are licensed to prescribe medicine. It is presumptive and dangerous for an untrained visitor to try to diagnose and prescribe for the patient.

9. **Do not criticize** the patient's doctor or pastor.

Confidence in one's doctor is a large measure of the cure. The visitor may not like the patient's doctor and any criticism leveled against him may undermine the sick one's confidence.

This is equally true in respect to the patient's pastor. It is unethical to call a pastor other than the patient's minister and ask him to call upon the sick one. The visitor may think that his pastor is more capable and may request him to see the patient. In that event, the minister requested may make the call and find the patient's own pastor there at the same time. In a similar situation a pastor related, "When I called on Mrs. ——, I saw a minister standing by her bed praying with her. I did not know whether I should interrupt, wait, or walk away. I decided to wait and I asked him why he was making a pastoral call upon one of my parishioners."

It is just as unethical for a minister to call upon another pastor's patient as it is for a doctor to professionally visit the patient of another physician.

In another instance a middle-aged patient with no church affiliation desired an opportunity to profess faith in the Lord and receive the sacrament of baptism. In ministering to her, we decided upon a church that she would attend and join as soon as she was able. I called the pastor of that church and offered to introduce them.

In the meantime some of the relatives got busy on the phone once they heard that she had been baptized. As a result of their zeal she was visited by a Roman Catholic priest, a Baptist minister, and a Pentecostal pastor, in addition to the minister whom I had called. The next morning she was spiritually confused after a restless night and was, no doubt, sorry that she had ever mentioned religion. Her physician was angry over it because her temperature was elevated and and she was restless. As a result of this it was necessary to exclude all clergymen from her room except the one who was originally called. It is always presumptuous to call a clergyman without the patient's consent. It may be assumed that the patient's doctor and pastor are both doing an adequate job.

10. **Permit** the patient to talk.

The art of listening will be discussed in greater detail in a later chapter. Some visitors mistakenly think that the express purpose of their call is to be an entertaining conversationalist. Should the patient interrupt and start to say something, this visitor may caution, "Don't talk . . . you'll tire yourself . . . let *me* do the talking."

When the visitor does all the talking it generally centers on his own oft-rehearsed description of aches, pains, and other unpleasant things. In such instances the patient will not only be bored but may hope that the "visitation" will soon be over. It is not advisable for the visitor to burden the patient with a recital of other people's troubles. What, then, should be the subject of conversation if the visitor is cautioned against discussing his own or other people's troubles?

The patient should be given the opportunity to talk whenever there is any sign that he wishes to do so, and the choice of the subject should be that of the patient's preference. The patient may grasp readily at the opportunity, especially if the period of illness has been lengthy and the visitors few in number. The patient may be interested in certain mutual friends and welcome information about them. In that event the visitor may share whatever knowledge he or she may have.

If the patient is permitted to talk at least fifty percent of the time of the visit, it was a successful call.

11. **Do not probe** into the patient's sickness.

If the visitor asks, "What is the matter with you?" and the patient replies, "I've had surgery," and does not comment further, it is ill-advised to ask, "What kind of surgery?" The patient would have shared the nature of the operation if there was a desire to tell it.

In many instances the patients regard the nature of the sickness as a personal matter and do not wish their medical history to be a matter of public record. Other patients are willing and eager to relate the details of their operation. If the visitor is a good listener, the call will be helpful. However, it is nearly always inadvisable to probe. One can take it for granted that the sick person who wants the nature of his illness to be known will talk about it without prodding. People with cancer and women who have had an operation on the sex organs are usually hesitant about discussing it with a visitor.

8

12. **Prepare to leave** when the conversation lags.

A helpful sick call is usually a brief one, unless the patient wants to discuss some matter of specific importance with the visitor. When the caller remains into the period of recurring awkward silences, the call has already been too long, although it may have lasted only a few minutes.

13. **Get ready and go.**

When the visitor says, "I must go now" he should leave. It is usually very boring when the caller prolongs his exit, and hesitates in a last desperate effort to say a parting word. The patient's remark, "I wish you could stay longer," is the courteous expression of appreciation for a visit that has reached the point for termination. The benefit of any visit is quickly cancelled by the visitor who doesn't know when to leave. It is far better for the patient to wish that the visitor could have stayed a while longer, than to be bored with a call that should have been terminated when the caller arose to leave.

14. **Do not whisper** outside the patient's door.

When the visitor leaves it is not advisable to linger in the corridor and whisper to another person. The patient may overhear parts of the conversation and wonder if his condition is more serious than he is being told. A male patient in an oxygen tent heard a visitor outside his door whisper to another that he would probably have another attack that would be fatal.

Whispering about any subject, either in the room or

9

outside it, may cause the patient to be apprehensive because what is said cannot be understood. Conversation should be sufficiently loud to be heard. A patient will usually assume that any whispered conversation is about his condition, and that the whisperers do not want him to hear what they are saying.

Those who visit the sick should be mindful of the fact that the unconscious patient may hear what is being said even though he is unable to respond by word or a gesture.

15. **Tell to nobody** what was spoken in confidence.

While the layman is not a clergyman who hears confessions, in some instances the patient may want to confide in someone and the visitor may arrive at the opportune time for it. The sick one may seek the relief of sharing a stress in confidence.

It is not unusual to find that under the influence of medication, or in moments of fear, guilt, anger, or resentment, the patient may confide his innermost feelings more freely than under ordinary circumstances. In such a situation, the visitor may listen but is ethically bound to hold in strict confidence whatever might have been shared under the influence of a stress.

These are some of the rules that are offered as guide lines for effective calling on the sick. Russell Dicks once said to me, "If you do no harm, you are helpful to the patient."

2. *Crises and Stresses in Sickness*

It has been wisely said that from the patient's point of view there is no *minor* operation. Any sickness may reach the state of a crisis situation whether illness be considered as "serious" or not. Most people can adjust to a temporary interruption in the routine of living without a major disturbance in personality equilibrium. Some cannot. The success with which one adjusts to sickness depends upon many factors. These include: religious beliefs, feelings of security, education, age, financial resources, job security, and the feeling that one is loved.

MOMENTS OF CRISES

The crisis situations most frequently encountered can be expected when the patient—

Is told that hospitalization is necessary.

Faces an operation.

Must submit to an amputation.

Awaits the results of tests.

Is told that the disease is serious or incurable.

Anticipates a long convalescence.

Faces death and is aware of it.

When Hospitalization Is Necessary

Most people resist hospitalization. For a few the hospital offers a way of escape from unpleasant home conditions, from the annoying spouse, or perhaps it may provide an avenue of satisfaction for a martyr complex. The vast majority of people, however, seek to avoid admission to a hospital as a patient. Hospitalization brings with it a drastic change in routine, entrance into a strange new world, and entrusting one's care to strangers.

The hospital is regarded in our day and age as a place where patients go to be restored to health. There are those, however, who regard the hospital as a last resort, a place where people are sent primarily when the sickness is so serious that it cannot be treated at home or when death is near at hand. Generally, when the doctor urges that the patient must be hospitalized, his words are interpreted to mean that the sickness is more than ordinarily serious. This may be disturbing.

Before Surgery

Facing an operation is usually a crisis situation because it is new and threatening. Furthermore, it is quite normal to fear the unknown. Even those who have previously undergone an operation may be quite apprehensive about another one. The change in daily routine, the sea of new faces, and isolation from home, family, and friends require adjustments on the part of the patient. If one has not previously been a patient in a hospital, it is a new experience and most people do not anticipate a new, unknown, experience, such as an operation, with pleasurable feelings.

Loss by Amputation

When the operation calls for an amputation, even if it is only the removal of a joint of a finger, the patient realizes that he will never again be as he was. If it is a major amputation involving a leg, an arm, or a breast, there must be a major readjustment after it is healed. It may mean a new way of earning a living or the patient may wonder if it will make him or her unattractive to the spouse or to others. A hysterectomy may also be considered in the category of an amputation, for the patiently usually reacts to it in a similar way. If a hysterectomy is performed before the menopause the patient realizes that she cannot have any more children. She may even fear that it may hinder her from functioning as a wife. A childless woman who must undergo such surgery may find it very disturbing.

Awaiting Test Results

One awaiting the results of laboratory and X-ray examinations will usually be apprehensive until the final diagnosis is made. Most people fear the worst that can happen. In this connection it may be said that doctors, nurses, and clergymen may be more apprehensive than others because they know more about the dire possibilities.

When the test is a biopsy to determine if the tumor is benign or malignant there will be considerable uneasiness, although the doctor may say, "I'm quite sure that it is benign, but we want to be altogether sure." When the patient responds by saying, "I am awaiting

13

the verdict," the use of the word "verdict" is a clue to his anxiety and fear.

Reacting to Bad News

When the patient is told that the disease is serious or incurable, the first reaction is usually that of depression and hopelessness. If the disease is incurable but not fatal, there is hope. The diagnosis of diabetes is usually quite disturbing until the patient realizes that it need not be fatal. If the patient carefully follows the prescribed diet and medication, a normal life span can be expected. Here then is a physical condition with which the patient must learn to live, just as others must adjust to dentures, bifocals, and hearing aids.

However, when the diagnosis is a fatal disease such as cancer, Hodgkin's disease, or leukemia there will usually be a reaction of deep depression and hopelessness. But, the good Lord has made us capable of adjusting to almost anything. As the patient lives with the realization that the disease is fatal there is almost always a grain of hope that in this instance it will not be. The slightest improvement in the physical condition will generate some hope. For that reason, the spiritual and mental condition of the patient will vary from day to day and, toward the end, from hour to hour. In these situations resources of religious faith and beliefs are of vital importance to the patient's comfort.

The Long Road Back to Health

When the physical condition makes a long convalescence necessary, the patient's realization of the arduous road ahead may burden him with critical problems.

When one is severely injured and knows that the period of recovery will require several months to a year, major adjustments must be made in life patterns. In addition to the boredom of a protracted convalescence, there may be worry over finances, job security, child care, home management, and countless other important factors of life. Two of the most disturbing reactions to a long convalescence are loneliness and worry.

Point of No Return

The last crisis situation to be mentioned in this connection is facing death. In some instances when a patient is not critically sick but thinks that he is, the reactions are as intense as they would be for the critically ill person.

The person who is aware of the imminence of his death will react in the pattern that takes into account his age, religious convictions, economic security, and his emotional attachment to family and friends.

An aged person may be weary of the life struggle and when there are religious convictions and beliefs in the goodness and mercy of the Lord, the approach of death may be accepted as a release from the pain and weariness of this world.

At any other period of life spiritual adjustments must be made to accept the inevitable in order to be able to do it with a benign spirit. Almost all people have some religious beliefs although they may not be church members. They may use whatever religious resources they have to help them adjust to the thoughts about approaching death.

It must not be assumed that because an individual is

a believer and a faithful member of the chuch that he is thereby immune from the fear of approaching death. Consecrated people are usually very sensitive spiritually and realize more than others how much they are dependent upon God's grace and forgiving love. Religious upbringing tends to quicken the conscience. The same act that would not disturb a person with few religious convictions may become quite a serious problem with a conscientious one.

A Christian woman once placed a bet on a horse and won. Several years later when she became seriously sick and faced an operation, this gambling experience worried her. To ease her conscience she gave an amount of money equivalent to her winnings to her pastor for the church. Millions of people gamble without the least twinge of conscience, but this woman's conscience was sensitive enough to arouse feelings of guilt in the matter.

MOMENTS OF TENSION

There are various tensions that arise in these crisis situations. They may be classified as (*a*) anxieties and (*b*) negative emotions. The three anxieties frequently observed at times of illness are: guilt, fear, and regret. The five negative emotions most generally observed at the time of illness are: loneliness, self-pity, despair, moroseness, and rebellion. These moments of stress vary in intensity with each person and range from the mildly distracting to the acutely disturbing.

Guilt Feelings

As was mentioned previously some people are more sensitive to guilt feelings than others. Almost all people have some religious beliefs and convictions. Even those who never attend a church are exposed to religious thoughts through the printed page, radio, TV, and conversation. It may also be said that few people have lived such perfect lives that they have never, at some time or another, violated their convictions or beliefs. At the time of serious sickness, any moral deviation may spring forth from the subconscious and arouse feelings of guilt.

The Roman Catholic Church makes it more convenient for its members to resolve feelings of guilt through its sacraments of confession and penance. Protestants and Jews may address their prayers for forgiveness directly to God. If this does not satisfy or resolve the feelings of guilt, the believer may make voluntary confession to the pastor or rabbi.

In many instances, the lay visitor is the convenient person with whom to talk over the cause of the guilt. As was previously said, what is revealed in confidence must always be considered as confidential. The lay visitor may offer the patient the suggestion that the feelings of guilt be shared with the patient's clergyman. If the sick one has no church relationship the visitor may offer to call a clergyman.

A Time to Fear

In our culture we are taught that fear is cowardly and bravery is praiseworthy. Many people hesitate to express fears lest they be considered cowards. The fact remains that most people experience fear before an operation or as they await the results of tests.

The patient may try to camouflage feelings of fear with bold statements such as: "I'm going to surgery in the morning, but I'm not afraid," or "I don't know why people are afraid of an operation," or "I have confidence in my wonderful doctor so I'm not afraid."

The visitor may put the patient at ease by saying, "Many people are afraid, I know that I was. I am glad for you if you aren't." After this the sick one may feel more at liberty to give expression to any fears that he or she may have.

Reflected Regrets

In some instances, lying in bed with one's own thoughts as the only diversion may be an opportunity for some soul-searching. Rummaging in the attic of memory may reveal some neglect of loved ones, particularly in relation to one who has passed away. The patient may seriously regret words spoken in anger, or a kindness withheld, or an angry deed. These memories may generate regret.

Again, as with feelings of guilt, the best help lies in the direction of giving expression to the anxiety. When the patient wants to talk about regrets, the visitor should be willing to listen and not try to suppress the urge by the premature comment, "You have nothing to regret; you were wonderfully kind," and the like. A woman who was not permitted by her pastor to express her feelings of neglect of her mother, but was, instead praised, said later, "I wish I were half as good as he thinks that I am." His call did not help her, for she still was anxious with regrets he did not let her express.

Shadows of Loneliness

Of all the negative emotions, loneliness may become

he most distressing one. In its intense form it becomes
nostalgia or homesickness. "I want to go home," or "I
wish I could be home," or "My children need me," are
frequent expressions of lonely, homesick hospital patients. The briefest span of time may seem to be too
long when one is separated from loved ones.

"They will get along without you," is definitely the
wrong thing to say, because it is not true. In addition,
the patient does not want them to get along without
him or her. The sick one wants to be missed and
needed. It is far more helpful to the patient if the visitor
says, "They will get along as well as they can until you
are home again with them."

Older people, in particular, may become lonely. During a long sickness, or when a person is confined by
the handicaps of old age, friends may neglect to call,
thinking that there will always be time left in which to
do it. People in nursing homes, state hospitals, and
homes for the aged are often overlooked, and some are
entirely abandoned.

Members of "sick" committees should give these people preference in planning a schedule for visiting. Any
inexpensive gift such as a handkerchief, candy, or fruit
will be appreciated. A card signed by members of the
church group or organization will bring lasting cheer.

Loneliness may also generate worry. When one has
nothing more to do or to occupy the attention over a
long period of time, one can think of dire results that
can happen in almost any situation. Worry over the
welfare of relatives, of self, of finances, and the like
may become a major stress.

19

Byways of Self-Pity

Self-pity is another of the devils bred by loneliness. With more time than diversions, the patient may center the attention upon self. Thoughts of neglect may lead the patient to blame relatives, friends, doctors, nurses, pastors or others for a fancied lack of attention.

"I slaved for them day and night and now they can't even find time to visit their old mother."

"No one knows what I've gone through this last year. My husband's uncle died, and my daughter got married, I had a virus, and now on top of all that, this had to happen to me. Won't there ever be an end to it?"

"No one cares if I live or die. I'd have to be on my deathbed before anyone would do anything."

These, and like expressions, are the results of loneliness that has bred self-pity. If the visitor can arouse more pleasant thoughts in the mind of the patient, the call will be helpful. When the patient begins to think of some happy incidents or kindnesses shown, or even becomes interested in the welfare of others, the unpleasant mood might be terminated, at least for a time.

Rock Bottom Despair

Another negative emotion is despair or hopelessness. Often there are good reasons for this attitude, and when the patient wants to talk about it, it is helpful if the visitor will listen.

Whenever a patient is seriously sick, or the period of convalescence has been long, the visitor may expect to encounter moods of despair and hopelessness. This may particularly prevail when the sick one has abandoned any hope of recovery. In many instances people have to live with a disease or an impairment, indefinitely or permanently. In the process of adjusting there will be moods of despair.

It is not helpful for the visitor to try to counter the mood with a joke or jokes. Some visitors think that a funny story is always appreciated in a sick room. The telling of a joke may actually cause a despairing patient to seethe with anger. The sick one is in no mood for laughter and may resent the visitor who minimizes the seriousness of his situation with wit and humor.

In most situations, when the disease is incurable or terminal there will be moods of despair and hopelessness when one's religious resources are about the only help available in addition to the support and prayers of friends or relatives. It should be said that during this mood the interest shown through a visit by a friend or a representative of the organization may be very helpful.

Dispelling Gloom

Moroseness and rebellion usually accompany each other. These negative emotions may plague the person who for years has been self-sufficient, but is now primarily or totally dependent upon others. It is rarely helpful for the visitor to commiserate with the patient in such mood. Rather, a serious effort should be made to help restore the patient's sense of dignity.

The patient may rebel against God, or loved ones, or anyone who genuinely tries to help. This is evidenced in the remarks made by an elderly woman with a fractured pelvis. When her pastor called she told him, "You can talk to me all you want to about a God of love,

21

but I won't believe a word you say. How could God do this to an old lady like me?"

A business man with multiple sclerosis said, "I hate for these people to stand there saying one thing when I know they're thinking, 'You poor devil, I feel sorry for you, but you have it coming to you.'"

The visitor can be helpful to the morose and rebellious patient by asking his or her opinion of matters, or by asking advice from the sick one. If the patient is wealthy the visitor may call a worthy cause to the attention. To talk over organization projects usually helps to restore dignity.

In conclusion, it may be said that these are the stresses and negative emotions that the visitor who calls on many sick people may encounter. It is not advisable to argue with a person, or to be overly solicitous. The friendship expressed in the act of calling is usually helpful and almost always appreciated. If the patient expresses gratitude and asks the visitor to come again, it may be assumed that the call was helpful.

3. *The Art of Listening*

Listening may be defined as the ability of one person to permit another to talk upon a subject chosen by the other one. It may be said that of all self-disciplines, the art of listening is one of the most difficult to master. Once it is mastered it becomes a highly rewarding accomplishment.

Many people like to talk, mostly about themselves; few people have learned to listen. One outgoing man always interrupts what anyone is saying with, "That's fine. That's fine—now let me tell you. . . ." He scarcely ever listens to anything anyone says. A friend confronted him and started rather sadly to say, "My mother-in-law passed a——."

"That's fine, that's fine," he interrupted. "I was going to tell you. . . ."

This man fancies himself to be adept at calling on the sick. In point of fact, he wearies the patient with trivial matters and monologue.

Your Visit Shows You Care

Rapport or empathy is essential to a helpful call. A visitor can scarcely ever be beneficial to a person who dislikes him.

The first few moments of any visit are crucial in determining the course and the effectiveness of the call. The visitor may find a clue to the patient's attitude with the earliest exchange of words. The rules of chapter one contribute toward empathy between the visitor and the one upon whom the call is made.

Establishing rapport seems to come more easily with some people than with others. Personality reflects sincerity, faith, love, tact, and other healing emotions. When the visitor has these, somehow they are communicated and the patient responds with friendly appreciation.

A young, inexperienced pastor became concerned about one of his parishioners who was a chronic complainer and continually sick. The pastor suspected that there was no organic basis for her illness. To verify this, he consulted with her family physician who confirmed his suspicion. The doctor said, "Reverend, there's nothing wrong with her but selfishness. If she'd get busy in the church, the Red Cross, or just do anything for other people and quit thinking about herself, she would be fine. You tell her."

The physician was correct in his diagnosis but wrong in his suggested method of cure. The inexperienced pastor followed the doctor's orders! To say that thereafter she thoroughly disliked the pastor would be an understatement.

He realized his mistake and tactlessness and tried to compensate for it with further friendly calls, attempting to regain her confidence. His efforts were, however, in vain. It would have been better for her if he had apologized, offered his services and stayed away, because after each call she was resentful and talked to a neighbor about him and his clumsiness. By generating resentfulness he was harmful to her. He deserved her attitude. However, the fact remains that rarely can one help another person unless there is a spirit of friendliness.

4 4 7 4 9

When the visitor and patient know each other personally a friendly and receptive attitude on the part of the patient may be anticipated. If the patient is a casual acquaintance or completely unknown to the caller, it is essential that early in the meeting the basis for a friendly relationship be established.

Tactlessness can strain even the most friendly attitude.

"I wish Mrs. —— would stay away," a woman patient said. "She always tries to pry into our affairs. And whatever you say to her you might as well publish in a newspaper."

A male patient said regarding two women who visited with him and prayed over him, "Those women from my wife's church always act like I'm not good enough . . . and I guess I ain't. They think they're the only ones going to heaven, and if they are, I don't want to go there. They can be as mean as the devil."

Calls such as the two foregoing ones are wasted efforts and do harm to the patient. Both of these patients disliked the callers and there was no rapport or empathy.

Upon entering the sick room the visitor should identify himself or herself. If the call is being made as a representative of a group or organization, it should be stated.

After the introduction the visitor will, most likely, inquire "How are you?" It is a habitual greeting, but in this instance it will be received by the patient as a serious inquiry. Under ordinary circumstances one does not expect a detailed account of the physical and/or emotional condition. When visiting the sick, however,

Lincoln Christian College

the caller should be prepared to listen. The patient may relate all the particulars about the current condition, the diagnosis and the prognosis. Or, if the patient is not feeling very well, may say, "I don't feel well today. How are you?" In either situation the patient will usually respond to the visitor, "How are you?"

This poses the first major hurdle for the visitor to overcome. The patient really does *not* expect the visitor to answer the greeting with a description of aches, pains, and ailings. At this point many visitors cannot withstand the temptation to talk about themselves.

"I had the same operation two years ago. The doctor said, etc., etc."

"My asthma has been acting up again. Last week Wednesday, no it was Thursday . . . yes, it was Thursday, I thought it was going to be the end. I managed to get to the phone, etc., etc."

Others who cannot overcome this first hurdle are those who know that they should not weary the patient with their troubles, but at the same time, want to enlist the sick one's sympathy. These may respond to the patient's "How are you?" in a manner such as this:

"I'm fine, but my poor mother! You know she is getting old now and can't remember. It's pitiful. Yesterday morning she came hobbling into the kitchen and said, 'Agatha, when are you going to take me to see ——?' and, I said, 'Why, mother, I took you there last week.' The poor thing just can't, etc., etc."

When the visitor talks about self or tries to enlist sympathy, there is an attempted exchange of roles: the patient becomes the listener, the visitor becomes the patient. The visitor should muster sufficient self-control

26

to master the first temptation to talk about self, and say, "I am fine, thank you. I want you to know that I am thinking about *you*. I wondered how you are getting along." If this can be done, the call is off to a good start; rapport is established if the patient likes the visitor.

However, there is never a rule without some exceptions. A pastor called frequently upon a shut-in, elderly lady parishioner. He never could master how to begin the visit satisfactorily. He tried in vain to break himself of the habit of saying, "How are you?" when he entered her home, because her reply always was, "How do I look?"

If he said, "I think you are looking better," her response was, "How could I? I feel terrible." If he said, "I think you are not looking so well today," she would answer, "I don't see why I shouldn't, because I'm feeling better." He never learned to greet her by merely saying, "Hello, Mrs. ———." In the first encounter the visitor can state in a friendy manner why the call is being made. He may begin with a permissive statement such as, "I wondered how you are getting along." The patient is then at liberty to talk and may choose the subject of the conversation. In response to the patient's remarks the visitor may follow the leads given. If the patient indicates directly or indirectly that he wishes to talk about some particular subject, and the visitor reacts favorably, the patient will lead to it.

Helpful Ways to Listen

The chief instrument of listening is the question. There are two methods of listening: active and passive.

In *passive* listening, the visitor serves in the role of a

recording device. The listener's ears are, in effect, the microphone into which the patient speaks. A patient may desire to talk freely, and express whatever may be on his mind. The visitor serves the purpose of a listening post. The listener's most important words in passive listening are, "Uh-huh," or "M-m-m," with an occasional affirmative nod of the head. Such responses require considerable self-control on the part of the visitor.

Passive listening can be therapeutically helpful for any person who is in stress and wants to talk about it, or for one who just wants to talk. Some of the most helpful calls a visitor can make consist of lending a sympathetic ear so people can unburden themselves.

In *active* listening the caller uses the question. The patient may say, "The doctor tells me I am getting along very well. I hope that he is right."

Visitor: Is there some doubt about it in your mind?

The patient's words, "I *hope* that he is right" indicate some doubt about his recovery. The visitor's question offers the patient an opportunity to express any thoughts about it if there is a desire to do so.

If the visitor had countered the patient's doubt with a positive statement such as, "Your doctor knows best," the visit would have been terminated. The patient would not have been given a chance to tell or talk about the reasons for the doubt.

Another patient may say to a visitor from his church, "I'm glad you came. You are the only one from the church who has taken the time to come!"

Visitor: Has our pastor called on you?

Patient: No he hasn't. I guess he's too busy.

Visitor: I wonder if he knows that you are sick.

Patient: I'm sure someone has told him. Someone usually does.

Visitor: May I call him and tell him about you?

Patient: You may if you want to.

If the visitor had countered her statement about neglect by the members of the parish or agreed with her, the matter would have been concluded. Offering to help, she asked permission to call the pastor. The visitor felt that the minister was unaware of the parishioner's hospitalization and rather than argue with her, offered to call him. When the minister visits her he may tell her why he did not come sooner.

A common statement made by patients who are women and have dependents is, "I'll be glad when this is over and I can return home again. They need me."

Visitor: I am sure that they do. Who is taking care of the children while you are here?

This mother is concerned about her family and does want to express her feelings. However, as was said previously, the visitor must be careful not to reassure the mother that the family is getting along just as well without her. By asking about the care of the children, the visitor encouraged the mother to talk about them if she desired.

By the use of the question and being permissive the visitor can usually be helpful.

If the patient does not wish to talk or is too sick to want to carry on a conversation, the visitor should not stay. The call has been helpful because the sick one knows that the visitor cared enough to make the effort to come. In such a situation the visitor may greet the patient and frankly say, "I do not want to weary you,

I will come again when you are feeling better," or "I just wanted you to know that I am thinking about you."

Or, the visitor may express good wishes for a speedy recovery and extend greetings from the organization that he or she represents and leave. If the sick one is asleep or indisposed the visitor may leave a card or a written note.

Avoid Making Judgments

The third important discipline to be mastered in listening is to be non-judicial or non-judgmental. This approach is not as complicated as it appears to be, for it merely requires the visitor not to express personal judgments and opinions too readily.

A patient said to a visitor, "Do you think it is right for our church to promote bingos?"

Visitor: I don't think it's wrong. The Bible doesn't condemn gambling.

By expressing an opinion too readily the visitor closed the conversation. Although the patient had qualms of conscience about promotion of bingos by the church, the opinionated, judgmental attitude of the visitor discouraged her from expressing her views.

If the visitor had, instead, answered the patient's query with the question, "What is your opinion?" conversation may have developed along the following lines:

"I think that it is wrong. . . . I've been taught that it is wrong. I attended one of those affairs, but after it was over I returned home and felt that I had sinned."

Visitor: Did you talk with our pastor about this?

Patient: I did. He said that there is nothing in the Bible that condemns it.

Visitor: But you feel that it is wrong?

Patient: Yes, I do. I can't tell you why I feel that way about it.

Visitor: Did you say you were taught that it is wrong?

Patient: I was raised in a Methodist church. Maybe you don't know this; I am a "convert." My people were terribly opposed to it. I'm not sorry that I changed, but it's difficult for me to accept some of the things I've been taught are wrong.

Visitor: Why don't you stay away from the bingos? The church doesn't say that you have to attend them, does it?

Patient: They don't say you have to attend, but I know the church needs the money. That's why they have them.

Visitor: Would it make you feel better about it if you contributed in cash what you usually lose?

Patient: I haven't thought of that. It's a good idea. I hate not to help the church. I know they need the money.

Visitor: Then you wouldn't feel bad about it.

As you study this conversation you will observe that the visitor did not answer the patient's question, "Do you think that it is right for our church to promote bingos?" The patient was not primarily interested in the visitor's opinion in the first place. In a situation such as this the visitor's view is not important. If the visitor had expressed her opinion by replying, "I don't see anything wrong with it," the patient would have dismissed the subject without a solution for her problem. If the visitor had replied, "I agree with you—it's wrong for the church to do that," the patient would still be left with the problem.

When the visitor had gone, the patient still did not know whether her visitor was for or against bingos. The private views of the visitor didn't really matter. Through her wise use of questions she helped this patient by suggesting that a cash contribution be made instead of her on-the-spot participation in a church-sponsored activity that caused her qualms of conscience. Although the patient had not thought of such a possible solution, she was pleased to make the suggestion her own.

Avoid Reacting to Shocking Statements

Guard against any appearance of shock or dismay at statements made or questions asked by the patient. Some people can be very frank, particularly when they are sick and fearful. When a patient asks, "What do you think of a person who would do . . .?", the visitor may have a strong opinion on the matter and be inclined to say so. Instead, the visitor should reply cautiously, "I really wouldn't want to say offhand, etc."

Patient: What do you think of a married woman who would get a crush on a married man?

Visitor: I really don't know offhand. I'd have to know more of the details before forming an opinion. Do you know anyone who has? Why do you ask?

Patient: This woman, you wouldn't know her because she doesn't live here, got a crush on a married man. She used to drive downtown mornings just to see him when he went to work at a store. He was a buyer for the store. She said they never met anywhere, but she would go to the store, make purchases, and ask a clerk about him.

Visitor: In cases like that they usually manage to meet somewhere. What makes you so sure they didn't?

Patient: She told me. I believe her. Once she tried to meet him in Indianapolis. He went there on a buying trip, and she found it out from a clerk . . . even the hotel where he was staying. So she told her husband she was going to Indianapolis to do some shopping and would stay overnight. She went to the same hotel where he was. She was going to call him and meet him in the dining room. She said she knew it was wrong, but she just wanted to do it. So, she bought a pint of whiskey. She thought if she'd drink a little it would give her courage. Have you ever heard of anything like that?

Visitor: There are a lot of things I haven't heard about. But what happened?

Patient: She must have drunk too much of the whisky . . . and she fell asleep. When she woke up it was three in the morning and she had a terrific headache. Then, she said, she realized what a fool she was making of herself. In the morning she took the first bus back home. But she has worried over it ever since.

Visitor: Does she still go to town mornings to see him?

Patient: My goodness, no. It's all over now. But it worries her terribly.

Visitor: I wonder if her husband knows about it.

Patient: I doubt it. She wouldn't tell him how silly she acted. Do you think she should?

Visitor: I'm not a marriage counselor. But if she is that worried about it why doesn't she talk with someone who could help her? I notice that Ann Landers, every once in a while, suggests to her readers that they talk over their marital problems with a clergyman.

Patient: If she ever mentions it to me again, I'll suggest that. But come to think of it, I don't believe she belongs to a church.

Visitor: Why don't you suggest to her that she talk with our pastor?

Patient: If she mentions it again, I think I will.

If, at the very beginning, the visitor had acted shocked at the idea of a married woman getting a crush on a married man and said, "I think that is terrible," the patient would have changed the subject. In this instance the caller exercised much self-control and was helpful. The patient was permitted to tell the story.

There is no way of knowing for certain who the penitent woman is, but, most likely, she is the patient who was talking. The visitor did not act shocked or opinionated, neither did she intimate any suspicion if there was any.

The caller provided additional assistance when she suggested talking with a pastor. If the woman is sincerely worried, whether she is the patient or another, she should find relief for her guilt stress and the pastor may help her with the problem. It should be noted, also, that the visitor was modest and frankly said that she was not a marriage counselor. There would probably be much less discord if amateurs did not regard themselves as experts in the area of marital counseling.

In some instances the patient may shock the visitor in reply to the greeting, "How are you?" with a disturbing diagnosis.

Visitor: How are you?

Patient: I just received terrible news. The doctor tells me I have cancer and you know what that means.

Visitor (calmly): Yes, that is serious, as you say. And it's bound to disturb you. Is he going to operate?

Patient: He's trying now to get me on the surgery schedule.

Visitor: What does he say about it?

Patient: He says that it is not too far advanced and he thinks that he can get all of it. But, I think he's just telling me that to make it easier.

Visitor: Who is your doctor?

Patient: He's Dr. ——, but he wants Dr. ——, who is a specialist, to do the surgery.

Visitor: I've heard a lot about him. They say that he is a wonderful surgeon. I doubt that your doctor would tell you it's not too far advanced if he didn't mean it. Isn't that right?

Patient: I'm told that he's quite honest with his patients. It's my only hope that he is. I'm glad he told me, though; I'd just as soon know as not know.

Visitor: I doubt very much that he would have told you if he did not think you could be healed.

In this confrontation the visitor handled the situation very well. When the patient said at the beginning, "I have cancer" the visitor's first reaction could have been, "Oh, . . . that's too bad." If that had been the response, the patient would have been further depressed by the shocked attitude of the caller.

The visitor was also helpful by supporting the patient's confidence in the doctor. Many cases of cancer that were incurable a number of years ago are now healed by surgery and therapy. The visitor did not try to minimize the seriousness of the situation, nor propose what the patient should do. Instead, the sick one's hope for recovery was supported by the visitor. Undoubtedly, the patient was grateful for this call.

In contrast, a retired man who visited for his church called upon a twelve-year-old member who was in a hospital. The child's mother was in the room with the child at the time of his call. In such situations the adults usually do the talking, the patient is ignored and listens. This visitor was curious and wanted to know what was wrong with a twelve-year-old girl. (It was none of his business. Curiosity is not a legitimate reason for a visit.) After an exchange of greetings and irrelevant remarks about weather and the attendance last Sunday, he noticed that the mother was not minded to divulge the nature of the girl's sickness.

Visitor: I sincerely hope she's getting along well.

Mother: It's not too serious. It was nice of you to come. If you have time, come again.

Visitor: If I can be of any help, let me know.

Mother: We will. Thank you.

Visitor: Will she have to have an operation?

Mother: No.

Visitor: Then I guess she's getting some kind of treatment. Is that it? Of course, I don't know what the trouble is.

Mother (in desperation): No or yes. All that happened was she was walking on a fence, fell, and hurt herself.

Visitor: Oh, my, I hope she's not permanently injured.

Mother (arising): Goodby!

This was a very harmful call. Any visitor may take for granted that when a patient refuses to talk about the nature of the sickness there is a reason for the attitude. A person's sickness is not a legitimate reason for anyone to pry into the nature of it. That is solely the business of the physician who is the professional helping person on the case. If a patient wants to talk about his illness, the visitor should be permissive in his approach.

In this instance, the injury was of too personal or intimate a nature to discuss it with a stranger, particularly a male visitor. When the visitor hinted that he wanted to know about it and said, "Of course, I don't know what the trouble is," he was exercising poor judgment or an erotic interest. He could not have done anything about it anyway.

When the mother told him that the girl would soon be better and thanked him for calling, he should have left. He antagonized the mother by pursuing the subject of the daughter's illness. In order to get rid of him, she finally told him. When she did, his shocked reply to the effect that he hoped she was not permanently injured was tactless and tasteless. In addition, though he completely ignored the one he came to visit, the patient heard all that was said.

This mother should complain to church authorities. This man should not be permitted to represent the church in calling upon the sick. In fact, this visitor is not spiritually healthy.

Be Spiritually Healthy

One must have faith in God before one can communicate it to others. In some situations, communication is not so much a matter of words as it is of bearing and behavior. The visitor's poise reflects inner beliefs. If the visitor believes that God's will for man is good, and that he desires that man's existence in this world be wholesome, healthful, and redeemed, such beliefs will be reflected in a friendly attitude and permissive approach.

The visitor's motivation in making the call will have much to do with listening ability. When the visitor calls for selfish reasons, such as to show what a good person he or she is, or because of any personal glory that may be derived from the good work, or because there is nothing more interesting to do, it is unlikely that the patient will be helped. Indeed, the patient may be harmed by such a visit. Under these conditions the visitor is primarily interested in self, not in the welfare of the sick one. In all probability this visitor will do the majority or all of the talking, and mostly about self and selfish interests. The patient's needs will be ignored.

When the motivation for calling on the patient is to express love, fellowship, and concern, the visitor is much more likely to negate self and selfish interests and to give the patient, should he so desire, an opportunity to do most of the talking. When this attitude is dominant the patient will have a much better feeling about the call which has been made.

Conclusion

It is not the purpose of this chapter to teach the visitor how to become an accomplished counselor. This skill cannot be acquired as easily and quickly as this chapter can be read and studied. When accepted and practiced, the five principles of the art of listening as discussed here briefly will assist the visitor in being helpful to the patient. The patient does not expect the lay visitor to be a counselor with professional skill, just a good listener and friend.

4. *The Art of Reassurance*

While the question is the primary instrument of listening, the positive statement or an affirmation is the important medium of reassurance.

"You are getting better."

"You will soon be fine."

"You will recover."

"God has forgiven you."

"God bless you."

"I know when you are well again you will attend church."

"You are a fine person. You have nothing to worry about."

All of these are positive statements of reassurance and they will be most meaningful to the patient if they are not spoken prematurely. A statement of reassurance is ineffective when spoken by the visitor too soon and glibly. The patient may conclude that the visitor either does not know the facts or is trying to deceive him.

Most visitors are so eager to be helpful that they do not hesitate to be dishonest. The visitor who seeks to comfort a dying patient by saying, "Don't talk like that. You will get well," is being dishonest and usually the patient knows it.

After the sick one has told the visitor that he knows

he will not recover, the caller may reassure with words similar to these, "I do not know if you will recover or not. Many have, and many have not. But God cares and has something to say about this also. His will is important and he loves us. You may rest assured that he loves you and will care for you."

A patient may demean himself or herself with a statement similar to this: "I know that I have not been an angel by any means. I could have done a lot better than I did."

Visitor: You aren't as bad as you think you are, so forget it now and get well.

Patient (to another visitor who came later): I wish I were as good as Mrs. —— thinks I am.

The first visitor was too anxious to reassure the patient who wanted to talk. If the visitor did not have time to listen she might have said, "No matter what the past has been, God gives us a chance to do better. I'm sure all of us could improve in our conduct." This reassurance may have strengthened the sick one's resolve and relieved some of the tension.

Most, if not all of us, have spiritual resources that may be drawn upon when facing and enduring sickness. Some people have developed more spiritual reserves than others. Other people may have neglected to fortify themselves spiritually for any stress that may develop beyond the toleration limit.

We automatically resist experiences that make us feel unpleasant. We can face up to an unpleasant situation without undue stress until it becomes so intense that we reach our toleration limit. This breaking point varies with individuals. In the process of adjusting to illness we may use whatever spiritual resources are available. It may be said honestly that all people have at least some spiritual resources, including those who do not profess a faith and do not belong to a church. A hospital chaplain who was ministering to a semiconscious, delirious "wino" observed that occasionally the dying man would mutter, "O God, O God." In his delirium he would raise his hand to his mouth as he did with a bottle of wine and go through the motions of drinking from the imaginary bottle. When the chaplain recited the twenty-third psalm to him there must have been moments of lucidity, for the man feebly said, "O God. O God."

No one knows what adverse conditions of our culture, society, or nature proved to be so overwhelming that he turned to alcohol for support. Perhaps, as a lad, his parents were not interested in his religious development. He may have grown up outside the influence of organized religion. But, somehow or somewhere he must have come into contact with religion and the church. Unfortunately, he did not develop sufficient spiritual resources or have the necessary professional assistance or intelligence to help him overcome his addiction to alcohol.

During moments of sobriety this alcoholic must have given God some thought. He may have tried to pray in his own way for help, but it was too late. During his final hours, rejected and alone, except for the doctor, nurses, and chaplain, in a haze of semiconsciousness he tried to call to God for help as best he knew how. It can be said that almost everyone has at least some measure of spiritual resources.

In contrast, a lady in her late sixties lay in bed shaking with the palsy and her body twisted with arthritis. By most peoples' standards, she had plenty about which to complain. Instead, she greeted each visitor with a smile. She said, "I have so much to be thankful for. The Lord is good to me. He gives me strength and courage to live one day at a time. I am not afraid because he is with me (indicating her heart) right here."

This woman has developed a tremendous tolerance for sickness and pain. Undoubtedly the forces that have made this possible for her are her spiritual resources.

In calling upon the sick the visitor will encounter people with varied spiritual assets. People with sufficient spiritual resources can adjust to almost anything and emerge from the process with mental and emotional equilibrium. In adjusting to sickness (or any calamity or misfortune) there are many spiritual resources that may be used to maintain health.

It may be said that a man's total personality is composed of mental, emotional, spiritual, and physical factors. All of these are interrelated and are mutually influential. Physical disorders influence the spiritual, mental, and emotional aspects of man's wholeness. In like manner, mental, emotional, and spiritual disturbances may affect physical health.

The visitor who can assist the sick one in using whatever spiritual resources may be available is helpful in restoring health and wholeness.

A table of spiritual resources that may be used by the individual who is sick or troubled and the tensions that may be relieved by them approximates the following design:

Faith versus fear, guilt, revenge, hostility, insecurity
    and worry
Sense of joy versus revenge, encourages forgiveness
Love versus hostility, loneliness, ingratitude
Dignity versus inferiority, rejection, anger
Hope versus despair, depression, guilt, sorrow
Courage versus fear, pain, uncertainty
Creativity versus boredom, self-pity, moroseness

FAITH

Faith is used here as including confidence in man as
well as God. The person who distrusts others, doubting
their honesty and sincerity, can become cynical, anxious,
fearful, and resentful. Untrustworthy people are in the
minority; most people are honest and sincere.

A male patient remarked to a visitor, "All preachers
are crooks." This visitor, representing the patient's
wife's church was not shocked by the statement. Pre-
vious callers from the church had been amazed by the
man's attitude and had not returned. This visitor replied, "You evidently have a reason for saying that.
Would you tell me about it?"

Patient: Sure! I know what I'm sayin'. There was a
preacher of your church who was no good. One day the
guy was missin' and all the church's money was missin'
with him. They haint heard from him since. He was
a crook.

Visitor: How long ago was that?

Patient: Oh, I don't know. Maybe ten years.

Visitor: You are right! I've heard about that. I guess
he was a crook. I've been a member for about seven
years now. The minister we now have has been with us

five years and he is a fine, Christian man. Have you ever met him?

Patient: He came here to see me but I told him all preachers are crooks. He didn't know what to say. He knows I'm right, so he said, "You want me to pray with you?" And I said, "No." He haint been back.

Visitor: You wanted him to argue with you, is that it?

Patient: No. Why should I?

Visitor: That's what I'd like to know. Surely you can't believe that because one preacher is a crook they all are.

Patient: That's what I said. All preachers are crooks.

Visitor: This one is not. But if you want to go on believing that, it is your privilege. The reason I called is that I want you to know that we of the church are thinking about you and feel kindly toward you. Goodby.

Patient: Hm-m-m. Goodby.

This was a difficult call for the church visitor. There was far more to the patient's antagonism and hostility than was revealed. It is unfortunate that this man did not have professional psychiatric help. There was some deeper basis for his hostility than the fact that one preacher ran away with the money. He had feelings of hostility toward all the members of his wife's church. His physical recovery was a long, slow process. He, most likely, will never be "well" or "whole" as long as he nurtures this cynical attitude.

In contrast, confidence in other people—the doctor, the nurses, the pastor, and friends—can be helpful to the patient's recovery. There is a very practical reason for this statement. People usually like to do things for those who appreciate kindnesses. This applies to doctors, nurses, friends, and loved ones. A cooperative and appreciative patient is easy to be nice to and will receive more attention and help than a cynical, hostile one.

Trust in others is a necessary part of health and wholeness. A physician wants the confidence of his patient. If a doctor must temporarily assign his patient to another one, he will seek to inspire his patient to have faith in the new doctor.

The same may be said when a new pastor comes to a congregation. He knows that he cannot be helpful if the people do not have confidence in him. If their loyalty is toward the former pastor, the incumbent will need to be patient and with his demeanor gain their respect.

It may be said that any visitor who disturbs a patient's confidence in the doctor, the nurses, or the pastor is not being helpful.

While faith in man is important, of still more significance is faith in God. Beliefs about God vary with individuals. If one believes that God is a harsh taskmaster who enjoys punishing people for their sins, this belief will not be helpful to a sick person. It might be helpful to one who has strayed far afield in sin. The fear of God may motivate a sinner to repentance and a more useful way of life. The fear of the Lord is the *beginning* of wisdom, but not all of it.

Belief in God's goodness, mercy, and love will assist the sick one in overcoming fears, guilt, anxiety, worry, and feelings of insecurity. However, some people regard sickness as a punishment for sin. "What have I done that God should punish me like this?" is a question often asked. Some pain and suffering may be the result of personal sin. If one is injured in a brawl, or hurt in an auto accident because the car was being driven at excessive speed, one might regard the suffering as a result of personal sin.

It is far more helpful, however, to regard suffering as a discipline rather than a punishment. When suffering is used in a creative manner to teach patience, love, confidence, sympathy, or any other helpful attitude, it is a discipline. Faith in God's redeeming love will strengthen the individual to accept it and make it personally beneficial.

The highest form of reassurance is the comfort that may be derived from God's Word, religious literature, and prayer. The patient may want such reassurance from a lay visitor and if there is an indication of such desire the visitor may use the following passages of Scripture:

It is for discipline that you have to endure. God is treating you as sons; for what son is there whom his father does not discipline? For they disciplined us for a short time at their pleasure, but he disciplines us for our good, that we may share his holiness. For the moment all discipline seems painful rather than pleasant; later it yields the peaceful fruit of righteousness to those who have been trained by it.

—Heb. 12:7, 10-11

More than that, we rejoice in our sufferings, knowing that suffering produces endurance, and endurance produces character, and character produces hope, and hope does not disappoint us, because God's love

has been poured into our hearts through the Holy
Spirit which has been given to us.

—*Rom. 5:3-5*

A Prayer for Confidence

To Thee, O Lord, who dost love us
We commend ourselves and our loved ones.
Thy love is greater than our own,
So it is with confidence that we commend to Thee,
Ourselves and those who are near and dear.

In the daytime and in the night
Let Thy guardian angels hover near;
Protect and defend us from all evil,
And keep us in Thy care.

Increase our faith, that we may rely
Upon Thy love, now and always.
Remove from our minds
Any undue concern, for we trust in Thee.

With this reliance, grant us, O Lord,
Calm and quietness in Thee.
Give us rest and healing
In body, mind, and soul,
And peace within the heart. Amen.

JOY

The Apostle Paul has been referred to as the "re-
joicingest person" in the Bible. "Rejoice, again I say,
rejoice" seems to be a theme of his life.

It is easy enough to tell a person to rejoice or have a sense of joy, but the message and the condition are not identical. The acquisition of a right spirit within is more likely to come about when one has reasons to be joyful. Any person who has faith in God and man and the accompanying feelings of security, forgiveness, and peace, has reasons to rejoice. A sense of joy helps one overcome feelings of revenge and encourages a forgiving attitude.

A male patient, in his forties with a nervous disorder was visited by his "boss." After the employer left, the patient said to a visitor, "He stood there looking at me and said he was sorry to see me sick. And I thought to myself, 'You liar. You're not sorry at all. I'm here because you put me here. I hope some day it happens to you and when it does I won't say, "I'm sorry," I'll say, "I'm glad you got, for once, what you deserve." ' " This man harbored feelings of revenge against his boss, and, most likely his attitude contributed to his nervousness, especially if he nurtured this tension over a long period of time.

A sense of joy does not mean that the individual has to surrender himself to bad treatment without protest. Anger, in itself, is not evil. It becomes harmful when one permits it to dominate one's mind with hostility and thoughts of revenge. On the other hand, a person with a sense of joy can accept the foibles of human behavior without being unduly disturbed. He understands and is willing to forgive, on the basis of his understanding.

"I want to apologize for the way I acted toward you the other day when you came into our office and talked with Mike," a man said to another at a service club luncheon.

The other: I don't quite understand what you mean?

Man: When you came in to talk with Mike, I didn't speak to you.

The other: I noticed that you didn't. But I thought you had a reason for it.

The man: Mike and I were talking when you came in. For a moment it made me angry when you interrupted us.

The other: Such things irritate me, too, at times. I don't blame you so please think no more about it.

Through his own experience the other man could understand, overlook an intended injury, and forgive it.

A sense of joy enables one to see the brighter side of an otherwise unpleasant experience. A middle-aged successful business man recovered from a serious sickness. As he was about ready to leave the hospital he said to a visitor, "This sickness has humbled me. I never realized how thoughtful people can be and how many friends I have until this happened. I am glad it happened. It was not pleasant, that is sure, but I learned a lot. I think I can truly say that now I feel kindly toward every person I know."

This man used his suffering creatively to cleanse his soul of ill-feelings, ingratitude, and revenge and replace them with a sense of joy.

Scripture has many references to joy. Some of them are as follows:

Thus says the Lord,
   your Redeemer, the Holy One of Israel:

"I am the Lord your God,
>who teaches you to profit,
>who leads you in the way you should go."
>>>*—Isa. 48:17*

Sing to the Lord a new song,
>his praise from the end of the earth!
Let the sea roar and all that fills it,
>the coastlands and their inhabitants.
Let the desert and its cities lift up their voice,
>the villages that Kedar inhabits;
let the inhabitants of Sela sing for joy,
>let them shout from the top of the mountains.
>>>*—Isa. 42:10-11*

As the Father has loved me, so have I loved you;
abide in my love. If you keep my commandments,
you will abide in my love, just as I have kept my
Father's commandments and abide in his love. These
things I have spoken to you, that my joy may be in
you, and that your joy may be full.
>>>*—John 15:9-11*

Rejoice in the Lord always; again I will say, Rejoice. Let all men know your forbearance. The Lord
is at hand. Have no anxiety about anything, but in
everything by prayer and supplication with thanks-
giving let your requests be made known to God. And
the peace of God, which passes all understanding,
will keep your hearts and your minds in Christ Jesus.
>>>*—Phil. 4:4-7*

A Prayer for Joy

All thanks to Thee, O Lord our God,
For all Thy marvelous works.
Thou dost bow down and hear us
When we are weak in sin.
Thou dost hear our pleas
And deliver us from our troubles.

Forgive us, O Lord, for neglecting Thee
In our thoughts, words, and deeds.
Fill our hearts with the joy of Thy salvation
That we may rejoice all our days.
Cleanse the mind of any evil thoughts
Toward anyone
That we may always be at peace
With Thee and our fellowman.
Through Christ's redeeming love. Amen.

LOVE

Love is a virtue that helps dissipate thoughts of hostility and ingratitude and dispels loneliness. As with faith, love may be a spiritual tie that binds a person to fellowman and God. When one is sick, afflicted, or in trouble one may doubt whether God cares at all. Many people have struggled with doubt, and during the struggle they have had a transforming experience that assured them that he does love.

If the visitor finds the patient in a mood to doubt God's love and care, the caller should not conclude that the sick one is being irreligious or does not believe. There can be no doubt without an element of belief. In most situations of this kind the love of God and for God does prevail in the believer's heart and faith is strengthened rather than weakened by the ordeal.

Love is a sustaining force in life, especially in sickness. Pain, delirium, nausea, and weakness are stresses that man experiences alone unless he knows that God is near and through his great love shares the experience. In time of stress the thoughtfulness of loved ones and friends is also a sustaining force that encourages the patient. Their remembrances warm the heart and are a healthy influence.

Patients usually respond to indications of love with a similar attitude toward others. Many people, when they are well, harbor some animosities and are often ungrateful toward those who do the most for them. In some instances they become angry with others whom, they think, are neglecting them, or talking about them. This attitude may particularly apply to older people. However, animosities and ingratitude are not confined to any age group.

Many sick people have experienced a change of heart toward others whom they previously disliked. The love that was shown to them caused them to realize that love is a healing force and negative emotions are not only harmful but, most likely, have no basis in fact at all.

It should also be said that love may dispel loneliness. Through the privilege of prayer man can experience the presence of God, who is awake while man is asleep, and who is near when man turns to him. In addition, thoughts about friends and what the patient will do for them when health is restored helps to keep the sick one mentally busy.

God has revealed his love for us in his Word. Men who were inspired by the Holy Spirit have recorded in Scripture what love did for them.

For God so loved the world that he gave his only Son, that whoever believes in him should not perish but have eternal life.

—*John 3:16*

Beloved, let us love one another; for love is of God, and he who loves is born of God and knows God. He who does not love does not know God; for God is love. In this the love of God was made manifest among us, that God sent his only Son into the world, so that we might live through him. In this is love, not that we loved God but that he loved us and sent his Son to be the expiation for our sins. Beloved, if God so loved us, we also ought to love one another.

—*I John 4:7-11*

Love is patient and kind; love is not jealous or boastful; it is not arrogant or rude. Love does not insist on its own way; it is not irritable or resentful; it does not rejoice at wrong, but rejoices in the right. Love bears all things, believes all things, hopes all things, endures all things.

—*I Cor. 13:4-7*

A Prayer of Love

O Lord, our Savior, we come to Thee
With a grateful heart, for Thy redeeming love
Has touched us also.
Each day the beams of the sun cover the earth
To give it light, warmth and life.
So is Thy love a redeeming force in life;
We feel its light, its warmth, its life.
Grant that we may reflect it
In our attitude toward Thee,
And those who minister to our needs,
And our loved ones, and all mankind.
When we are lonely, O Lord,
Be Thou near
To comfort and guide us
In the way that we should go. Amen.

DIGNITY

One of the serious hazards of sickness is ego-injury. The ego always tries to protect itself. When it is injured it may respond in any of a number of ways of expressing feelings of rejection or inferiority or anger. For that reason the visitor should respect the sick person's dignity. Just because a person is physically sick is no reason to assume that the patient is also mentally or emotionally ill.

A prominent business man developed multiple sclerosis. He continued to go to his place of business. His employees liked him and he tried to be a good Christian man. One day, as he attempted to walk up a stairway, he missed a step and fell. A young employee saw the mishap and ran to his assistance. To the young man's dismay and humiliation the employer looked up, cursed him, and said that he was quite able to take care of himself. His changed attitude puzzled the employees.

This man was accustomed to helping others, to having his own way. As the sclerosis progressed he became increasingly sensitive about it, particularly when people sympathized with him and tried to assist him. His dignity was challenged and his ego injured. Unfortunately, he became more gruff with people, except those who treated him with dignity and let him take care of himself as best he could. Those who asked his advice or help were treated very kindly. His physical condition did not affect his mental ability to make wise decisions in regard to business matters until much later when he was almost completely incapacitated. Even in that condition, his top associates continued to ask his advice. Although they did not always follow his advice, they were sufficiently wise not to tell him so when they did not.

An otherwise normal person may be offended by affected and undue sympathy. Only hypochondriacs thrive on sympathy. Others want to be treated with dignity. It is better to permit and even encourage a sick or handicapped person to do as much for himself as he can without too much discomfort. For that reason, hospital patients are invited by Red Cross Gray Ladies and occupational therapists to make and do various things. Patient activities encourage self-respect and preserve dignity.

Many well-meaning but thoughtless or tactless visitors do a tremendous amount of ego-inquiry with questions or statements which should be avoided. The following are frequent comments in sick visitation.

How old are you? (Should not be asked of anyone other than children and perhaps those over eighty who may be proud of their age.)

You've worked hard enough. You should take it easy now. (No one wants to be a has-been.)

When are you going to retire? (The patient may not be old enough to retire and should be permitted to make the announcement personally when the time comes.)

The business can get along for a while without you. No one is indispensible. (Most people like to think that they are indispensible and some are.)

You mustn't try to do that. You know you can't. (Let the patient try again. Perhaps it can be done.)

It is amazing how many visitors can be tactless enough to ask, "How old are you?" When this question is asked of a middle-aged woman she will most likely reply, "How old do you think I am?" Such a response places the visitor in a quandary. If he or she realizes that the query should not have been asked, in the reply the visitor may subtract about ten years from the guess and becomes a liar. If the visitor answers the patient's question honestly, the sick one will be offended.

When a middle-aged man is asked, "How old are you?" he may reply, "I am thirty-nine." That should be sufficient hint for the visitor to forget the matter, but if it is pursued the patient may say, "It is none of your business," or state an age in years. But the answer should not be taken seriously.

When a visitor is foolish enough to pry into a patient's age the answer should be a foolish one also.

Questions and statements by visitors that may support the patient's dignity are:

Has the doctor told you when you can be back on the job . . . go home . . . go back to school?

We miss you and hope you will soon be with us again.

Do you remember the old saying, "Try and try again?"

You have done a good job with that pot holder . . . painting . . . needlepoint. It is very pretty.

We need your advice. Do you think we ought to . . . ?

The place isn't the same without you, so hurry and get back.

I know your family will be glad when you are home again.

Anything that the visitor may ask or say that will make the patient feel wanted, needed, and loved will be helpful. These are basic human desires.

The Scripture abounds with references to human dignity. Our blessed Lord considered people so important that he was willing to suffer and die for each one's individual redemption. He enforced his support of human dignity with parables, such as the parable of the lost coin (Luke 15:8-10), the lost sheep (Luke 15:4-7), and many other sayings.

"Therefore I tell you, do not be anxious about your life, what you shall eat or what you shall drink, nor about your body, what you shall put on. Is not life more than food, and the body more than clothing? Look at the birds of the air: they neither sow nor reap nor gather into barns, and yet your heavenly Father feeds them. Are you not of more value than they? . . . But if God so clothes the grass of the field, which today is alive and tomorrow is thrown into the oven, will he not much more clothe you, O men of little faith?"

—*Matt. 6:25-26, 30*

What then shall we say to this? If God is for us, who is against us? He who did not spare his own Son but gave him up for us all, will he not also give us all things with him? Who shall bring any charge against God's elect? It is God who justifies; who is to condemn? It is Christ Jesus, who died, yes, who was raised from the dead, who is at the right hand of God, who indeed intercedes for us? Who shall separate us from the love of Christ? Shall tribulation, or distress, or persecution, or famine, or nakedness, or peril, or sword? As it is written,

"For thy sake we are being killed all the day long; we are regarded as sheep to be slaughtered."

No, in all these things we are more than conquerors through him who loved us. For I am sure that neither death, nor life, nor angels, nor principalities, nor things present, nor things to come, nor powers, nor heights, nor depth, nor anything else in all creation, will be able to separate us from the love of God in Christ Jesus our Lord.

—*Rom. 8:31-39*

A Prayer for Dignity

Dear God, our Father;
Thou has created us in Thy image
That we may know and love Thee.

Through Thy Son, Jesus Christ, our Savior,
Thou didst redeem us
And make us joint heirs with Him
Of all Thy love and care.
Help us ever to remember
That we are Thy children,
And help us to be worthy
Of our high calling.
Give us a full measure of Thy Spirit
That we may think and act
As Thou wouldst have us do.
In Jesus' name, we pray. Amen.

HOPE

The patient may use the spiritual resource of hope to dispel despair, depression, guilt, and sorrow.

There are times when the best way to master the present is to look ahead to a brighter future. It is not an easy matter to assume this posture when pain and uneasiness of body, mind, or spirit make minutes seem like hours. But the time always comes when the present experience will be an incident of the past. Looking ahead serves as a bright star in the night that lifts our vision above and beyond the present moments.

Then, too, hours or days of sickness may teach the patient to wait upon God. In that way they help the sick one to grow into a mature spiritual person. The patient inspired by hope will have more patience to await God's healing forces.

Even though the body has served its purpose in this world, there is always a tomorrow. God's plan for human life reaches beyond the physical span of life in terms of three-score years and ten. God's design for man reaches into a glorious eternity.

However, most people want to live in this world as long as they can, and therefore they want to have hopes of getting well again. Under no circumstances is it the visitor's prerogative to tell a patient or intimate that there is no hope for recovery. There is no certain way of knowing that a patient will or will not recover. If the visitor thinks the patient should be told because the sick one is an unbeliever or has refused the sacraments it is not advisable for the visitor to assume the responsibility of imparting the news. Whether the patient should or should not be told of the nearness of death is a matter that ought be decided by the doctor, the nearest of kin, and the spiritual counselor—not by a lay visitor.

It may also be said that a patient with a heart condition or leukemia should not be discouraged from marriage or work by a lay visitor. Such people have a right to enjoy, as much as possible, whatever months or years God may grant them in this world. When the light of hope is extinguished, the patient becomes deeply depressed.

When a patient is suffering with a guilt stress, hope for forgiveness is important. Through faith and sincere repentance it may be experienced. The visitor may help the distressed one to understand that God does forgive. In addition, the caller may suggest that the patient talk with a clergyman about it.

In deep sorrow there may always be hope for a reunion with the loved one in the eternal life. The believer is promised that there will be no more pain or sorrow in eternal glory (Revelation 21:1-4).

In conclusion, it may be said that the visitor will be helpful who encourages the patient to look ahead with a hope that sees beyond the shadows of the present moment to a brighter day that will surely come. The Scripture contains many references to hope, one of the great healing virtues.

> "The Lord is my portion," says my soul,
>   "therefore I will hope in him."
> The Lord is good to those who wait for him,
>   to the soul that seeks him.
> It is good that one should wait quietly
>   for the salvation of the Lord.
>
> —*Lam. 3:24-26*

> "Blessed is the man who trusts in the Lord,
>   whose trust is the Lord."
>
> —*Jer. 17:7*

> Behold, the eye of the Lord is on those who
>   fear him,
>   on those who hope in his steadfast love,
> That he may deliver their soul from death,
>   and keep them alive in famine.
>
> —*Ps. 33:18-19*

> "And now, Lord, for what do I wait?
>   My hope is in thee."
>
> —*Ps. 39:7*

We have this as a sure and steadfast anchor of the soul, a hope that enters into the inner shrine behind the curtain . . . .

—*Heb. 6:19*

For in this hope we were saved. Now hope that is seen is not hope. For who hopes for what he sees? But if we hope for what we do not see, we wait for it with patience.

—*Rom. 8:24-25*

So that we might be justified by his grace and become heirs in hope of eternal life.

—*Titus 3:7*

A Prayer of Hope

Thou art our hope and refuge in the time of trouble.
As the hart pants for the water brooks
So the soul longs for Thee.
When we are discouraged we find hope in Thee,
Thou are our comfort and strength in every need;
Thy promises of old are still true today,
When we turn to Thee, Thou dost lift us up.
Then, we can look ahead, we see afar, the way is clear
And we shall yet praise Thee
For all Thy goodness and mercy. Amen.

COURAGE

In the realm of the healing virtues courage comes very near in importance to the immortal triangle: faith, hope, and love. Faith, hope, and love are the roots that nourish the tree of courage. It may also be said that without fear and uncertainty there could be no courage. When there are conditions that make one afraid and uncertain, faith, hope, and love give the courage one needs to face them.

"I was taught and I believe that God takes care of his own," a widowed mother of four said. "When my husband died suddenly I was left penniless with four other mouths to feed and I was afraid. I prayed to God for help, for I needed his help and the encouragement of friends. I told him I would do my best. God gave me the courage I needed to find a job. I had never gone out to work before. And I want you to know that God has taken care of us, and with the help of my friends and employer we are getting along very well."

It must have taken a lot of courage to face the world with four children and no money. This woman had faith in God, and confidence in herself and others. Motivated by love for her children, she was able to provide for their needs.

When the patient is afraid and uncertain it is always better to admit it and talk about it with a friend, a clergyman, or a doctor. Since it is commonly believed that one should not be afraid, a sick person who is apprehensive may try to leave the impression that there are no fears. This does not help the situation. When the causes of fears are brought to light the individual may be assisted to face the present and the future with faith in God and confidence in self.

Courage lifts the soul. It will help the patient to recovery by giving an incentive to get well. It encourages planning for the future, and fighting spiritually to gain the victory. The Bible has many passages written to give courage. They should be read slowly and thought-fully.

And he said to me, "It is done! I am the Alpha and the Omega, the beginning and the end. To the thirsty I will give water without price from the fountain of the water of life. He who conquers shall have this heritage, and I will be his God and he shall be my son.

—Rev. 21:6-7

"Be strong and of good courage. Do not be afraid or dismayed before the king of Assyria and all the horde that is with him; for there is one greater with us than with him. With him is an arm of flesh; but with us is the Lord our God, to help us and to fight our battles." And the people took confidence from the words of Hezekiah king of Judah.

—II Chron. 32:7-8

Be watchful, stand firm in your faith, be courageous, be strong.

—I Cor. 16:13

Finally, be strong in the Lord and in the strength of his might. Therefore take the whole armor of God, that you may be able to withstand in the evil day, and having done all, to stand. Stand therefore, having girded your loins with truth, and having put on the breastplate of righteousness, and having shod your feet with the equipment of the gospel of peace; above all taking the shield of faith, with which you can quench all the flaming darts of the evil one. And take the helmet of salvation, and the sword of the Spirit, which is the word of God. Pray at all times in the Spirit, with all prayer and supplication. To that end keep alert with all perseverance, making supplication for all the saints, and also for me, that utterance may be given me in opening my mouth boldly to proclaim the mystery of the gospel.

—Eph. 6:10, 13-19

A Prayer of Courage

Thou, O Saviour, didst set Thy face
To go steadfastly to Jerusalem.
There Thou didst endure the cross,
Suffering and death,
And didst emerge victorious evermore!
When we are uncertain or afraid,
Give us the courage to set our face
Steadfastly to the present and the future.
No matter how many may be our afflictions
Thou wilt deliver us out of them all.
Grant that we may feel Thy strong arm
As it upholds and lifts us up
Into the clear air of courage
That the soul delights to breathe. Amen.

CREATIVITY

Sometimes we wonder how good can grow out of sickness. When we ponder the meaning of it all, we find that it can be creative. Does it make God more real? Does it help to see things in their right perspective?

Does it make the patient more appreciative of health and other blessings of life? Does it give understanding and sympathy?

Many emerge from sickness much stronger spiritually than they were before. In the stress of dark hours there is a tendency to re-examine those values in life that are important. Small, petty thoughts are then recognized for what they are. Trivialities become unimportant and the patient reaches a higher level of self-understanding and the purposes of life.

During the period of recovery and convalescence the patient may plan for the future and such creative thoughts can banish boredom and self-pity that otherwise idle moments can breed. When such measures of self-examination and discipline are taken, one is cleansed spiritually and mentally and sickness is being used creatively. The Bible reveals the ways in which suffering may serve noble purposes in life.

> He will deliver you from six troubles;
> in seven there shall no evil touch you.
> In famine he will redeem you from death,
> and in war from the power of the sword.
> You shall be hid from the scourge of the tongue,
> and shall not fear destruction when it comes.
> At destruction and famine you shall laugh,
> and shall not fear the beasts of the earth.
> For you shall be in league with the stones of
> the field,
> and the beasts of the field shall be at peace
> with you.

—Job 5:19-23

Thus says the Lord,
　　your Redeemer, the Holy One of Israel:
"I am the Lord your God,
　　who teaches you to profit,
　　who leads you in the way you should go."
　　　　　　　　　　　　　　　—Isa. 48:17

"And I will put this third into the fire,
　　and refine them as one refines silver,
　　and test them as gold is tested.
They will call on my name,
　　and I will answer them.
I will say, 'They are my people';
　　and they will say, 'The Lord is my God.'"
　　　　　　　　　　　　　　　—Zech. 13:9

A Prayer of Self-Examination

Our Father in heaven, as we look within
We see how often we have failed Thee
And our fellow men.
We have not always had the good of others at heart;
Nor have we always done the right
When we had opportunity.
Now, as we await Thy healing,
We have time to think on these things
And resolve to use our lives
In constructive, helpful ways.
Forgive us, we pray Thee
And support us in our determination
To live our lives closer to Thee
In love at home

68

And with purpose to do the right,
Through Jesus Christ, our Savior. Amen.

CONCLUSION

The purpose of this chapter is to help the visitor appreciate and understand some of the stresses that arise in sickness and the spiritual resources that may be used to face and counteract them. If the visitor is a good listener the patient may share some of these problems. The caller can be helpful by suggesting positive methods to the patient, if the patient asks for guidance.

5. *Visiting the Aging*

With the increase in the average life span the percentage of older people is higher than ever before and their number is likely to continue to increase in the years ahead. By 1970 it is estimated that there will be twenty million people over sixty-five years of age. Having added many years to the life span, professionals have done little to help the aging live their years of retirement in a creative and meaningful way. It has been estimated that twenty-five percent of those who reach the age of sixty in reasonably good health will develop chronic ailments during the following five years.*

Within the last decade the demand for rooms and beds for the aged and aging in nursing homes and homes for the aged has precipitated the construction of many such institutions by churches, fraternal organizations, private interests, and others. With all these added facilities the need and demand continues.

In addition to these agencies there are many state and private hospitals for mentally ill and senile patients as well as county homes for indigent elderly people. Many thousands of old people are receiving custodial care in these institutions and will remain there until they die. It may be said that in all homes for the aged, regardless of their nature and affiliation, there is a count-

* See Averill, L. A., and Kempf, F. C., *Psychology Applied to Nursing,* Fifth Edition (Philadelphia and London: W. B. Saunders Company, 1956), p. 359.

less number of forgotten aged people whose relatives or friends, if they have any, never call upon them or show any interest in their welfare. In many instances of such neglect relatives fear that if they show any interest in the aged relative the institutional, welfare, or family service officials might ask them to take the old person to their home so as to make room in the institution for another, or be held financially responsible for the care.

In one instance, for example, an elderly woman was brought from a "county home" to the hospital for medical care. She was "on relief." As the nurses were helping her dress for bed one of them noticed a bulge in one of her undergarments. An investigation revealed that she had about seven thousand dollars sewed in the black skirt. They informed the hospital administration who in turn summoned a deputy sheriff to witness the proceedings. The money was placed in the hospital vault, in her name, for safekeeping.

Later that day the chaplain happened to meet the township trustee who had admitted the elderly lady as a charity patient. The trustee remarked sadly to the chaplain, "I feel sorry for the old lady. She has relatives but none of them pay her any attention. When they are through with her here I'll have to take her back to the 'home' and she hates it."

The chaplain said, "I have an idea that after this evening's papers are out there will be plenty of relatives who will want to take her home."

"What do you mean?" the trustee asked.

"She is not a pauper," the chaplain explained. "A deputy was here today and my guess is that he will talk to reporters. Please trust me. If there is nothing about her in the evening papers, I think you have a right to know the story. My guess is that you will not have to take her back to the county home."

The deputy liked publicity and the chaplain's guess was right. The evening newspaper carried the story as did radio and T.V. and the deputy was the hero who found all the money and was holding it for her. As a result of the publicity any number of relatives quarreled among themselves regarding which one should have the privilege of taking care of the old lady. She did not suffer for lack of visits from relatives while she was in the hospital and did not have to return to the county home.

This is a sorry commentary on human nature, but those who are interested in the welfare of the aged might as well face reality. Most of the elderly have not had an opportunity or the foresight to provide financial security for their old age, although this picture is changing with the increase of pension plans and social security benefits. However, now and for many years to come, there will be many older people in homes, agencies, and institutions receiving custodial care who are forgotten or neglected by relatives and friends.

These are the people who really need, appreciate, and are benefited by the calls of visitors. When members of churches and organizations must retire to an institution it is vitally important that their names be kept upon the visiting and mailing list. Hospital patients generally have about as many visitors as they can tolerate, but these old people are usually neglected. A visit to one of them is appreciated more than the caller will ever realize.

In addition, an inexpensive gift is appreciated. A few oranges, bananas, some candy, a handkerchief, or a pretty card is kept and shown to anyone who will take the time to look and listen. It is highly recommended that members of "sick committees" who want to be particularly helpful devote their attention to old people in nursing homes, county homes, or who live alone and are retired.

Old people like to reminisce. The visitor who will take the time to exercise passive listening will be sincerely appreciated and helpful. A recital of events with which the visitor is not at all acquainted may be quite boring for the caller. But the end result is ample recompense for the boring experience, for the patient is helped and that is the reason for the call in the first place. If the visitor repeats calls upon the same elderly person it can be expected that the same stories will be told again and again.

One of the many plagues of old age is loneliness. So many lifelong friends have passed away and younger people have their own interests to keep them busy. Even if some relatives call as often as they can the old person may still feel neglected and complain that they do not come often enough. And, the visitor may be told, "It is so long since you were here I did not even know you when you knocked at the door."

Many older people will be dissatisfied, no matter what their living arrangements may be. Some are able to adjust to the infirmities of old age in a remarkable manner and graciously accept the fact that they need assistance from others. Most older people prefer to live in their own homes, even when they must be alone. Children are often criticized by outsiders for permitting an aged mother or father to live alone. But the elderly person should be allowed his or her independence as long as possible. The aged parents are not always happy in the homes of their children when, as is often the case, there is a lack of genuine understanding between the generations. The visitor may do well not to give advice on this matter, but permit the family to decide whether the aged one can or cannot live alone.

Some old people become very forgetful, or irritable, or imagine neglect on the part of others. Much of this may be caused by nature's normal process of the aging of body and mind. This should be accepted without resentment. It can happen to anyone.

The visitor may be helpful by listening but should not be judgmental and blame the relatives without first ascertaining the facts. When a visitor called upon an old man, his daughter, in whose home he lived, asked if the visitor would object if she used the opportunity to go to a store for some purchases. As soon as she left the house, the old man started telling the visitor how his daughter neglected him. He complained that she did not even give him enough to eat, left him alone, etc., etc. The visitor believed him until he said, "Look at my tongue." He stuck out his tongue. "There you see it," he said. "She drove a nail through my tongue this morning." Then the visitor realized that the old man was imagining his neglect. With nothing more to do than to live with his own thoughts, he pitied himself and imagined neglect until it became an obsession. He was living in a world of fantasy as many lonely old people do.

In conclusion it may be said that old people should

be treated with love and dignity no matter what the infirmities may be. They crave attention and love and the lay visitor may well give them priority on the visiting list and schedule. It should also be said that a lonely old person is not likely to expect a short call. The visitor may be prepared to stay a while and listen. It will be appreciated.

Appendix A
Literature for the Sick

Many visitors prefer to leave a reminder or a small gift with the patient. Some bring religious leaflets or pamphlets and leave one or more of these with the sick person. While some tracts and pamphlets may be very helpful, others can have a harmful effect. Leaflets that frighten the patient or threaten the sick one with hell or picture God as a cruel tyrant should not be given. "Where Will You Spend Eternity?" printed significantly in red, or "What If You Should Die at Midnight?" are the type of tracts that should not be given to seriously ill patients or those about to undergo surgery.

We recommend as helpful the following pamphlets and brochures:

Comfort and Strength, available from your church supply house, or directly from Eden Publishing House, 1720 Chouteau Avenue, St. Louis, Missouri, 63103. Upon request a sample packet will be sent, and the visitor may order the leaflets that are wanted.

Booklets of daily devotions (*Light for Today, The Upper Room, The Secret Place,* and others similar in nature) may be secured from denominational bookstores.

Healing Petitions, Comrades for Loneliness, Prayers for Quiet Hours may also be obtained from denominational bookstores. Attractive and inexpensive devotional booklets (*Greetings to the Shut-in,* edited by G. Waklin; *Thou Art with Me,* by D. Nystrom; *God is Our Refuge;* and *Prayers for the Sickroom*) may be obtained from any Lutheran Church Supply Store or from 2900 Queen Lane, Philadelphia, Pennsylvania, 19129.

The Reverend Ray Lanham, Associate Chaplain of the Methodist Hospital at Indianapolis, Indiana, and the Reverend Dr. Ruben J. Bierbaum, Associate Chaplain of the Deaconess Hospital of Evansville, Indiana, recommend the following:

Courage for Days of Illness by Edmond H. Babbitt is one in a series. Others are *Inspiration for Days of Illness* and *The Bible for Days of Illness.* These may be ordered from the Blodgett Press, Inc., Albion, Michigan, 49224.

God at My Bedside by Eugene L. Mendenhall, Jr. It may be ordered from Warner Press, Anderson, Indiana, 46012.

Strength for Hospital Days by Edmond H. Babbitt. This booklet may be ordered from The Board of Hospitals and Homes of the Methodist Church, 1200 Davis Street, Evanston, Illinois, 60201.

Grace Sufficient by Wayne E. Oates. It may be secured from The Broadman Press, 127 Ninth Avenue, North, Nashville, Tennessee, 37203.

There is other helpful and appropriate literature for the sick but any of these that are mentioned will be appreciated and helpful to the sick one.

Appendix B
Evaluating the Sick Call

It will be very helpful to both the visitor and the patient if the visitor will occasionally take the time to evaluate a call that was made. In grading there is a natural tendency to favor ourselves. If the evaluation is to serve its purpose we must try to be as objective about it as we can. When making the evaluation the visitor will profit by it if he or she will assume the role of the patient who was visited. From the viewpoint of the patient try to evaluate the call that was made as if you were calling upon yourself.

1. When I made the call, was the time of my call convenient for the patient? _____ Did I think about the patient's convenience? _____
2. Did I let the patient chose the subject of the conversation? _____ Or did I? _____
3. How much of the time did I talk about myself? Half? _____ A fourth? _____ Practically none? _____
4. How much of the talking did I do? Practically all? _____ A half? _____ A fourth? _____
5. How long did I stay? Too long? _____ Not long enough? _____ About right? _____

6. If I could not see the patient did I leave a written message? _____

7. Did I sit down before I was invited to? _____

8. Did I bore the patient with my problems? _____ The problems of others? _____

9. Did I criticize the patient's doctor? _____ The nurse? _____ The hospital? _____ The clergyman? _____

10. Did the patient want me to read and/or offer a prayer? _____

11. Did I insist on offering a prayer when the patient really did not want me to? _____

12. When the conversation lagged did I know I should leave? _____

13. When I said that I was going did I leave? _____ Stand and talk a while longer? _____ Be seated again? _____

14. Did the patient thank me for calling? _____ Say that my call was helpful? _____ Ask me to come again? _____

15. Did I tell anyone anything the patient told me in confidence? _____ What? _____
_____

16. How did I feel later about the visit? Good? _____ Bad? _____ Indifferent? _____

17. Rereading this evaluation, answered as honestly as I could, how can I improve the next visits I make? _____

The foregoing is a "soul-searching" evaluation and I doubt if very many would score perfectly on all the questions. If you were brutally critical of yourself and scored only one half of them as correct for your call the chances are that you were helpful by showing your love and concern. However, if you scored low on 2, 4, 5, 8, 9, and 15, your call was harmful, and you should try desperately to improve in these areas.

If you scored yourself perfectly on all of them, you are either one of a few of the perfect callers or you have overestimated yourself.

The purpose of this evaluation is to assist and encourage the visitor so that in making visits to the sick both the caller and the patient will have experienced a meaningful and helpful relationship.

INDEX

82

262.15
SCH 32

44749

3 4711 00195 3340